T0034881

THE
MAGNIFICENT
BOOK
OF
SHARKS

THE MAGNIFICENT BOOK OF SHARKS

ILLUSTRATED BY
Val Walerczuk

WRITTEN BY
Barbara Taylor

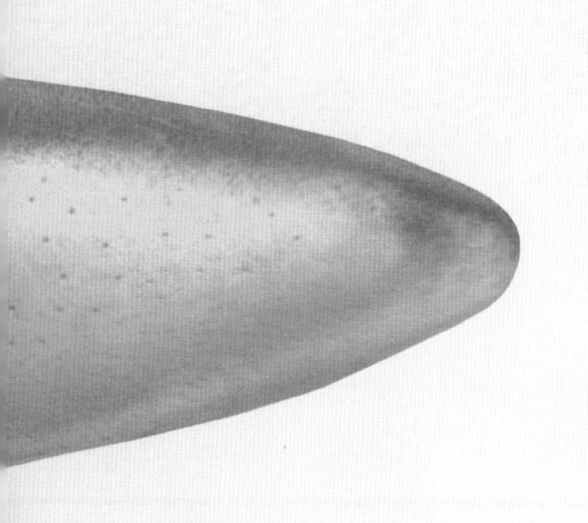

Written by Barbara Taylor
Illustrated by Val Walerczuk
Additional Illustrations by Simon Mendez

Published by Weldon Owen Children's Books
An imprint of Weldon Owen International, L.P.
A subsidiary of Insight International, L.P.
PO Box 3088
San Rafael, CA 94912
www.insighteditions.com

Weldon Owen Children's Books:
Designed by Bryn Walls
Edited by Diana Craig
Assistant Editor: Pandita Geary
Art Director: Stuart Smith
Senior Production Manager: Greg Steffen
Publisher: Sue Grabham

Insight Editions:
Publisher: Raoul Goff

ISBN: 978-1-68188-798-2
Manufactured, printed and assembled in China.
First printing, March 2022. LEV/03/22
26 25 24 4 5 6 7 8 9 10

Introduction

From wide-open seas to shorelines and shallow coral reefs, from sunlit surface waters to inky-black depths, sharks are at home in all the world's oceans. There are more than 500 different species of sharks. These prehistoric survivors have lived on our planet for around 450 million years, but today their existence is threatened by climate change, ocean pollution, and capture of sharks for their meat, skin, oil, and fins.

The Magnificent Book of Sharks takes you on an underwater journey to meet some of the most amazing inhabitants of the sea. Marvel at the gigantic whale shark—the biggest fish in the world—or the tiny pygmy shark, which is no bigger than an adult human's hand. Meet the great white shark with jaws that can slide forward to snatch its prey, and the sawshark, which slices through fish with the saw on its snout.

Meet a shark named after a Japanese goblin and another that barks like a dog. See the epaulette shark that can "walk" on land, and marvel at the frilled shark, which hasn't changed in millions of years. Discover which sharks like to hunt in packs, learn why some glow in the dark, and find out what mermaid's purses are.

Get to know all these fascinating facts and more on your unique underwater voyage through the magnificent oceans of the world.

Fact file

Lives: Worldwide

Habitat: Cold, temperate, and tropical oceans

Length: 15–20 ft (4.5–6 m)

Weight: Up to 5,000 lb (2,250 kg)

Life span: Up to 60 years

Diet: Large fish, seals, dolphins, small whales, sea turtles, seabirds

Contents

Great hammerhead

Sphyrna mokarran

- A great hammerhead shark is almost as long as a great white shark!
- This shark's wide head is shaped like a hammer. The "wings" on either side support the head in the water and allow it to lift and turn quickly.
- The great hammerhead can see a long way above and below its head. To see directly in front, it has to turn its head from side to side.
- The hammerhead's large nostrils give it excellent sniffing power, and help it follow the scent of prey in the water.
- The hammerhead has tiny holes, or pores, on its head. It uses them to pick up the electrical signals given off by its prey.

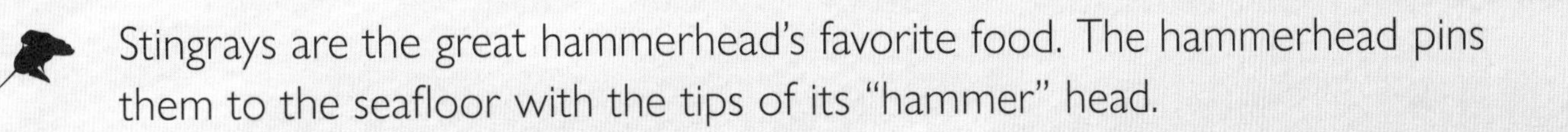

- Stingrays are the great hammerhead's favorite food. The hammerhead pins them to the seafloor with the tips of its "hammer" head.

- Shark babies are called pups. Female great hammerheads give birth to 13 to 56 pups, after a pregnancy of about 11 months.

- Newborn hammerhead pups are 20–28 in (50–70 cm) long. They will have to grow ten times as big to reach their adult size.

Fact file

Lives: Worldwide

Habitat: Coastal waters, coral reefs, open ocean

Length: 20 ft (6 m)

Weight: Up to 1,000 lb (450 kg)

Life span: 20–30 years

Diet: Stingrays, bony fishes, small sharks, squid, crabs

Blue shark

Prionace glauca

- Blue sharks are long-distance swimmers, migrating across oceans to find food or a mate.
- These sleek and speedy sharks sometimes use their long front fins to ride the underwater currents, like a surfer riding the waves. This helps them save energy.
- Rows of jagged, backward-facing teeth help stop a blue shark's prey from escaping. The shark also has fingerlike bristles on its gills to stop small prey from wriggling free.
- The blue shark has a white belly, a dark blue back, and bright blue sides. This helps camouflage it against the lighter sea above and the darker water below.

- Blue sharks often live in all-female or all-male groups. These groups include sharks that are about the same size, although the largest shark is often the leader.

- These sharks feed on almost anything, from squid and fish to seabirds and crabs. They've been known to eat trash, including plastic, which can make them sick.

- People hunt blue sharks for sport and for their skin, liver, and fins, which are made into shark fin soup. Up to 20 million blue sharks are killed by humans every year.

Fact file

Lives: Worldwide

Habitat: Temperate and tropical open oceans

Length: 12.5 ft (4 m)

Weight: Up to 450 lb (204 kg)

Life span: 20 years

Diet: Squid, octopus, fish, shrimp, lobster, seabirds, smaller sharks

Port Jackson shark

Heterodontus portusjacksoni

- The Port Jackson has a dark band across its body, which helps to break up its outline and disguise it from predators.
- This shark is commonly found in the harbor of Port Jackson in Sydney, Australia. It is also known as a pigfish or a tabbigaw.

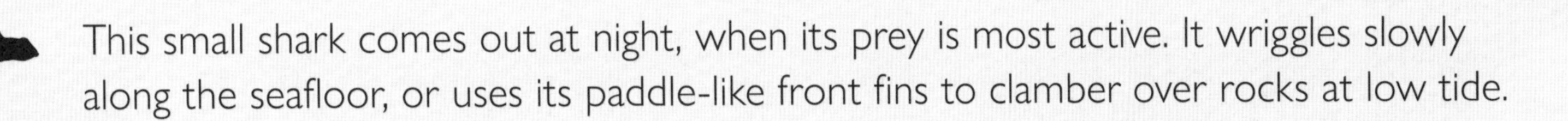

- This small shark comes out at night, when its prey is most active. It wriggles slowly along the seafloor, or uses its paddle-like front fins to clamber over rocks at low tide.
- The Port Jackson shark has two types of teeth. Its small, sharp front teeth hold and cut some of its prey, while its wide, flat back teeth crush hard shells.
- Unlike many other sharks, the Port Jackson does not need to keep swimming with its mouth open in order to breathe. It can breathe while it is lying still, which leaves its mouth free for feeding.
- The female Port Jackson shark lays spiral-shaped egg cases. The egg cases are soft at first to help her push them into rocky crevices, or hide them among seaweed.

Fact file

Lives: Southern and western Australian coastal waters

Habitat: Seabed near shore, caves, seagrass beds

Length: 2½–4½ ft (75 cm–1.37 m)

Weight: 13–99 lb (6–45 kg)

Life span: 10–30 years

Diet: Sea urchins, shellfish, crabs, prawns, sea stars, fish

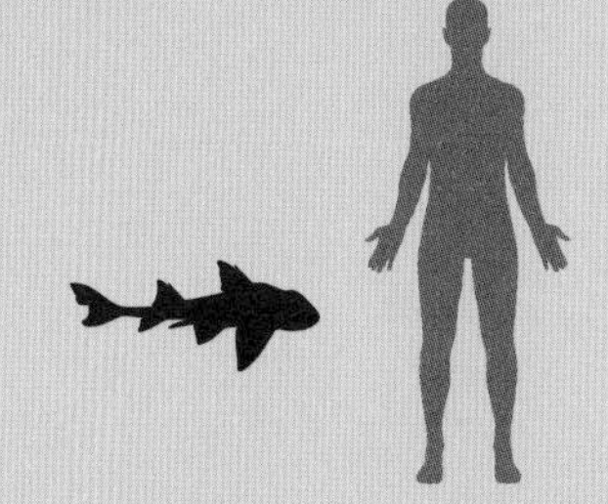

Great white shark

Carcharodon carcharias

- The great white is the biggest hunting fish in the ocean. It has no real enemies, except for orcas and people.
- A great white shark has up to 300 teeth in multiple rows. When a tooth wears out or breaks, it is replaced by the one behind it. The shark may use up to 30,000 teeth in its lifetime.
- The biggest teeth of a great white are as long as an adult human's finger.

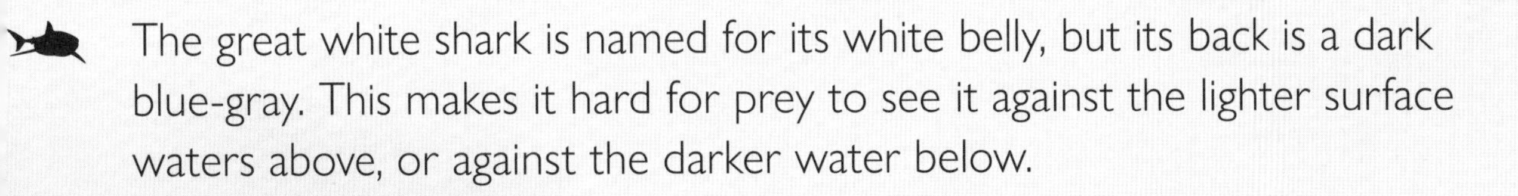

- The great white shark is named for its white belly, but its back is a dark blue-gray. This makes it hard for prey to see it against the lighter surface waters above, or against the darker water below.
- A great white can swim at the speed of about 15 mph (24 kmh), which is three times as fast as a champion human swimmer.
- This powerful hunter often attacks from below. It moves so fast that when it reaches the surface of the water, it cannot stop and shoots right out.
- A great white shark can take big chunks out of its prey. This is because its loose jaws slide forward so that they can open really wide when it is ready to bite.

Fact file

Lives: Worldwide

Habitat: Cold, temperate, and tropical oceans

Length: 15–20 ft (4.5–6 m)

Weight: Up to 5,000 lb (2,250 kg)

Life span: Up to 60 years

Diet: Large fish, seals, dolphins, small whales, sea turtles, seabirds

Velvet belly lanternshark

Etmopterus spinax

- The velvet belly lanternshark gets its name because its belly looks like soft, dark velvet. But like all sharks, its rough skin feels like sandpaper.

- All of the black patches on the shark's belly, sides, and fins glow blue-green in the dark. These patches are made up of glowing spots called photophores. One velvet belly lanternshark can have 500,000 photophores.

- Velvet belly lanternsharks use chemical messengers in their blood, called hormones, to switch their light spots on and off.

- This small shark lives far down in the darkness of the deep ocean. Large eyes help it see in the inky blackness.

- The shark's glowing belly makes it almost invisible to predators lurking below. They cannot see it against the faint rays of sunlight filtering down from above.

- The lights on the edges of the shark's fins shine through the transparent spines on its back. This makes the velvet belly lanternshark look as if it has sharp, glowing knives on its back. It's a warning to predators to stay out of its way.

- Velvet belly lanternsharks use their patterns of glowing lights to find each other. Males and females can tell each other apart using their glowing light signals.

Fact file

Lives: Eastern Atlantic Ocean, Mediterranean Sea

Habitat: Deep ocean

Length: 13–24 in (33–60 cm)

Weight: Up to 1.9 lb (861g)

Life span: 18–22 years

Diet: Small fish, squid, krill, shrimp

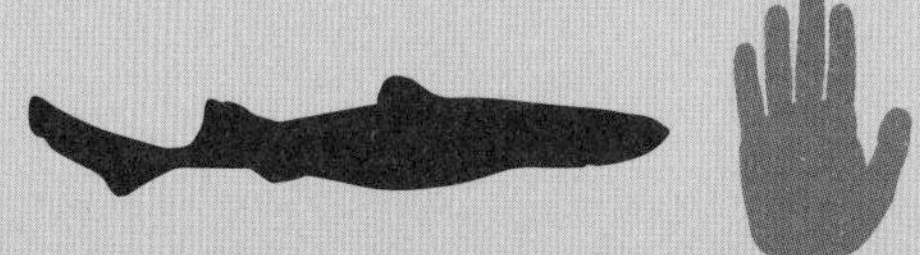

Coral catshark

Atelomycterus marmoratus

- The big, catlike eyes of the coral catshark help it see at night when it goes hunting.

- The coral catshark's long, slender body and short, flat snout allow it to find food in small spaces on a coral reef. Its spotted pattern helps camouflage it from both prey and predators.

- Large holes behind the catshark's eyes help it breathe when it is resting or feeding. It takes in water through these holes, known as spiracles. It pumps the water over its gills, which take oxygen from the water.

- Baby coral catsharks hatch out of purse-shaped egg cases. Long, curling threads on the corners of the cases help them cling to coral or seaweed so they don't get washed out to sea.

- This shark belongs to the huge catshark family. It has more than 100 relatives, which include the lollipop catshark, the spongehead catshark, and the white ghost catshark.

- Loss of its coral reef habitat, overfishing, and pollution all threaten the coral catshark. Some coral catsharks are caught for aquariums too.

Fact file

Lives: Eastern Indian Ocean and western Pacific Ocean

Habitat: Shallow water on coral reefs

Length: 1.7–2.25 ft (50–70 cm)

Weight: 1–2 lb (750 g–1.1 kg)

Life span: 10 years

Diet: Small fish, clams, crabs, shrimp

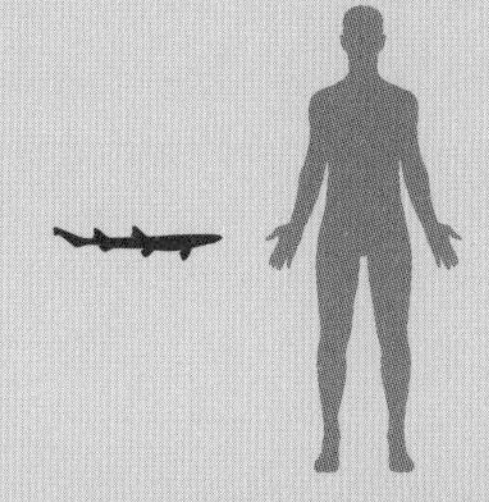

Silky shark

Carcharhinus falciformis

- The silky shark has especially smooth and silky skin.
- Like other sharks, the silky's skin is covered in tiny, toothlike points. These "teeth" are small, overlapping, and tightly packed together in silky sharks, which is why their skin is smooth.
- Silky sharks have an excellent sense of hearing. They can pick up the sounds of dolphins or birds feeding, which tells them where to find fish.
- Silky sharks are superfast swimmers and zoom after tuna at lightning speed. They sometimes get caught in fishing nets by mistake.
- Silky sharks work together to force small fish into tightly packed groups near the surface of the water. Then the sharks charge into these balls of fish with their mouths wide open.
- These large sharks are active, bold, and curious, and can be a danger to people. They will quickly attack if they feel threatened.
- Female silky sharks give birth to their young in coral reef areas. Here, there is plenty of food for the pups and protection from predators, such as larger sharks.
- Silky sharks may become endangered due to overfishing. They are caught by people for their meat, oil, skin, jaws, and fins, which are used to make shark fin soup.

Fact file

Lives: Worldwide in warm oceans

Habitat: Open ocean, rocky reefs, island coasts

Length: 7¾–12 ft (2.4 m–3.5 m)

Weight: 392–770 lb (178–350 kg)

Life span: 20–25 years

Diet: Tuna and other fish, octopus, squid, crabs

Nurse shark

Ginglymostoma cirratum

- The slow-moving nurse shark lives on the seafloor. It sometimes uses its strong front fins to creep over rocks and coral.
- Nurse sharks rest on the seafloor during the day. Up to 40 nurse sharks often sleep together, piled up in a big heap. This could help protect them from predators, such as lemon sharks or bull sharks.
- The barbels, or fleshy feelers, under the nurse shark's nose help it feel for its prey. When it finds a meal, the shark sucks in the food quickly.

Fact file

Lives: Atlantic Ocean, Pacific Ocean

Habitat: Shallow coastal waters, coral reefs

Length: 7½–10 ft (2.3–3 m)

Weight: 200–330 lb (90–150 kg)

Life span: 18–25 years

Diet: Crabs, lobsters, sea urchins, fish, shrimp, squid

- The nurse shark's mouth is like a powerful vacuum cleaner. It can suck a conch snail right out of its shell.
- This peaceful shark may bite a person if it feels threatened. A nurse shark's bite is very painful because its sharp, jagged teeth are like cheese graters. They help the shark grind up the hard shells of crabs and shellfish.

Pelagic thresher shark

Alopias pelagicus

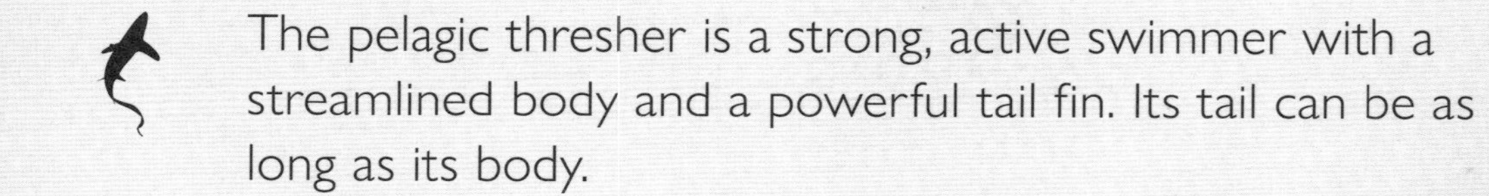

- The pelagic thresher is a strong, active swimmer with a streamlined body and a powerful tail fin. Its tail can be as long as its body.
- Pelagic thresher sharks sometimes jump right out of the water, like dolphins. This is called breaching.
- The thresher swims at high speed toward a school of fish, then it brakes sharply, slings its tail over its head, and slams it down to thresh, or beat, its prey.
- Despite their large size, pelagic threshers have a small mouth. They can only eat small prey, such as anchovies, sardines, herrings, and young tuna.
- Pelagic threshers prefer to swim in pelagic—or open—sea, rather than near the shore.

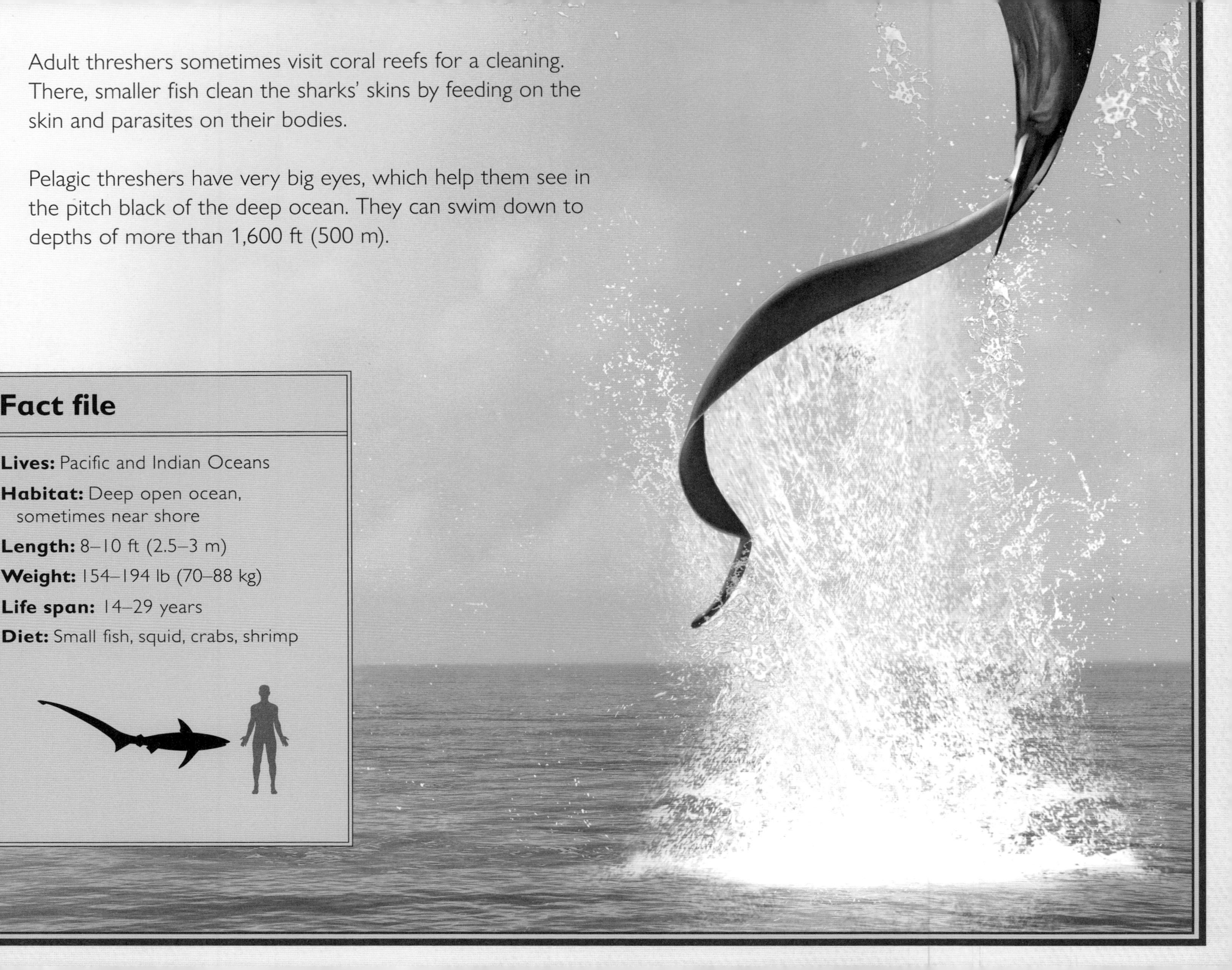

- Adult threshers sometimes visit coral reefs for a cleaning. There, smaller fish clean the sharks' skins by feeding on the skin and parasites on their bodies.

- Pelagic threshers have very big eyes, which help them see in the pitch black of the deep ocean. They can swim down to depths of more than 1,600 ft (500 m).

Fact file

Lives: Pacific and Indian Oceans

Habitat: Deep open ocean, sometimes near shore

Length: 8–10 ft (2.5–3 m)

Weight: 154–194 lb (70–88 kg)

Life span: 14–29 years

Diet: Small fish, squid, crabs, shrimp

Tasselled wobbegong

Eucrossorhinus dasypogon

- "Wobbegong" is an Australian Aboriginal word meaning "shaggy beard."
- The colored patterns and tassels on this shark's body help camouflage it from its prey. The tassels can also sense the movements of prey.
- This predator ambushes its prey at night. If any fish comes near its huge mouth, it strikes like lightning and sucks them up.
- This cunning shark sometimes waves its tail back and forth to look like a small fish. When other fish come to investigate, it snaps them up.
- The wobbegong's mouth is big enough to swallow other, smaller sharks whole.

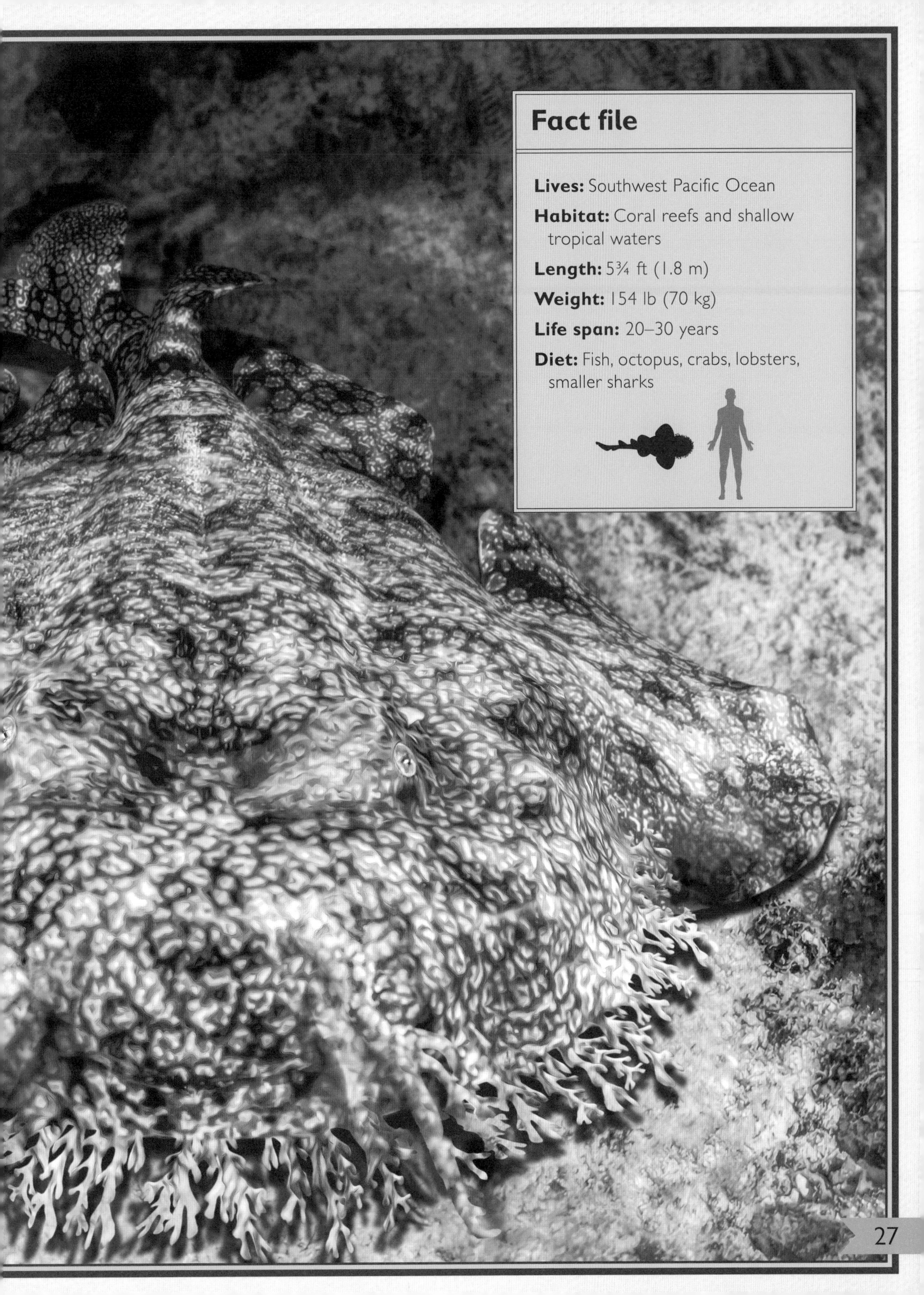

Fact file

Lives: Southwest Pacific Ocean

Habitat: Coral reefs and shallow tropical waters

Length: 5¾ ft (1.8 m)

Weight: 154 lb (70 kg)

Life span: 20–30 years

Diet: Fish, octopus, crabs, lobsters, smaller sharks

Spiny dogfish

Squalus acanthias

- Spiny dogfish hunt like packs of wolves. They work together in groups of hundreds or even thousands of sharks, rounding up schools of fish. Living in groups protects them from predators too.
- These sharks catch their prey using their strong jaws and sharp teeth. Sometimes they ram into their prey before they eat it.

Fact file

Lives: Pacific Ocean, Atlantic Ocean

Habitat: Coastal, surface, and deep water, river estuaries

Length: 3¼–4 ft (1–1.24 m)

Weight: 7–22 lb (3.2–10 kg)

Life span: 30–100 years

Diet: Fish, squid, octopus, shrimp, crab, smaller sharks

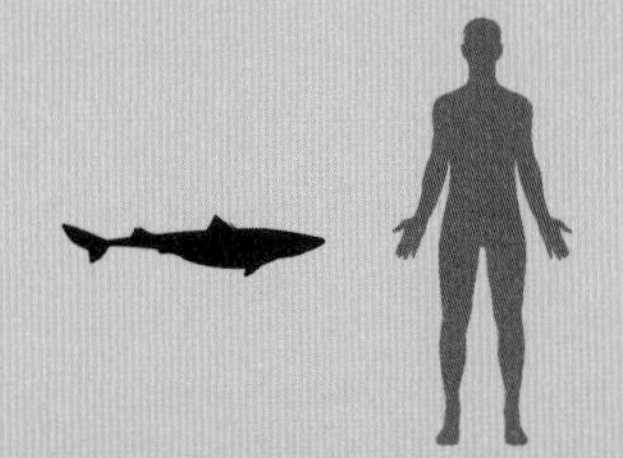

- The sharp spines in front of the dogfish's back fins are poisonous. The fish uses them to defend itself from predators, such as larger sharks, seals, swordfish, and orcas, also called killer whales.
- Female spiny dogfish develop more slowly than other sharks. They cannot become pregnant until they are at least ten years old.
- Spiny dogfish sometimes bite through fishing nets to steal the fish caught inside.
- The spiny dogfish was once one of the most common sharks in the ocean. Too many of them have been caught by fishermen. They are now in danger of extinction, especially because they take so long to produce their young.

Whale shark

Rhincodon typus

- The whale shark is the biggest shark of all, and the largest fish in the ocean.
- This giant shark eats tiny prey. It feeds on small fish and microscopic plants and animals, called plankton, that drift in the sea. It filters them out of the water using bristles on its gills.
- Using their gills, whale sharks can filter over 1,312 gallons (6,000 litres) of water every hour. That's the same as 33 bathtubs!
- The colossal mouth of a whale shark is up to 5 ft (1.5 m) wide. Its mouth lies at the front of its head, rather than underneath like most sharks.
- The whale shark has the thickest skin of any living creature. Its tough skin is about 4 in (10 cm) thick and feels very rough, like sandpaper.

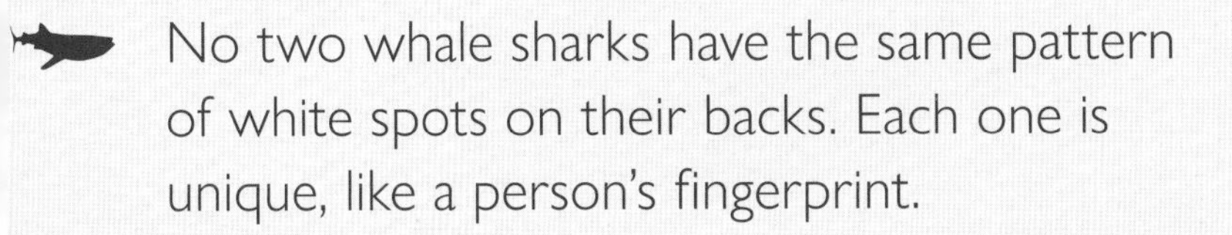

- No two whale sharks have the same pattern of white spots on their backs. Each one is unique, like a person's fingerprint.

- Despite its size, this shark does not sink when it feeds at the surface. Its huge liver is full of oil, which is less dense than water, so it helps to keep the shark afloat.

- Whale sharks are harmless and sometimes allow humans to hitch a ride by holding on to their fins.

Fact file

Lives: Worldwide, except Mediterranean Sea

Habitat: Temperate and tropical oceans

Length: 33–60 ft (10–18 m)

Weight: 47,000 lb (21,500 kg)

Life span: 70–100 years

Diet: Plankton, small fish, squid

Goblin shark

Mitsukurina owstoni

- The goblin shark has survived for millions of years in the world's oceans without changing very much at all. Scientists are still learning about this mysterious shark.

- Japanese fishermen were the first people to describe the goblin shark more than a hundred years ago. They named it after an imaginary Japanese goblin, called Tengu, that had a very long nose.

- The sluggish goblin shark has softer, flabbier skin than most other sharks. This may help it withstand the pressure of all that water above it in the deep ocean.

- Goblin sharks have see-through skin with lots of tiny blood vessels just under the surface. The blood shows through the skin, and makes it look pinkish.

- The flat, pointy snout of the goblin shark is full of sensors that pick up electrical signals from nearby objects. They help the shark find its prey.

- The goblin shark is not fast enough to catch speedy prey. Instead, it extends its jaws forward at high speed, right out of its mouth. The jaws move so fast that they can seize the prey before it swims away.

- Sharp, fanglike teeth at the front of the shark's mouth are used to grab prey. Smaller teeth at the back of its mouth are used for chewing.

Fact file

Lives: Pacific, Atlantic, and Indian Oceans

Habitat: Mid water to deep water

Length: 5–12½ ft (1.5–3.8 m)

Weight: Up to 460 lb (210 kg)

Life span: 20–60 years

Diet: Small fish, crabs, shrimp, octopus, squid

Blacktip reef shark

Carcharhinus melanopterus

- The blacktip reef shark usually lives around coral reefs. It swims in water so shallow that its triangular back fin shows above the surface of the water.

- This strong, athletic swimmer is one of the few sharks that can jump out of the water and spin in the air. It often does this when hunting fish that swim near the surface.

- Blacktip reef sharks usually hunt at night, and may work together to herd small schools of fish into one spot. They can pick up the electrical signals given off by prey, which allows them to find food in the dark.

- The blacktip reef shark threatens other sharks by arching its body, rolling from side to side, and opening its mouth. It also uses its tail to slap the water.
- If no males are around, female blacktip reef sharks can produce babies on their own. These pups are identical to their mother.
- Blacktip reef sharks sometimes push their noses above the water to look around. This is called spy-hopping.
- This timid shark is not usually a danger to people. But if it is frightened, it may bite the feet and legs of people wading in the shallow water where it lives.

Fact file

Lives: Pacific Ocean, Indian Ocean, Mediterranean Sea

Habitat: Warm, shallow coastal waters

Length: 3¼–6½ ft (1–2 m)

Weight: 43–55 lb (20–25 kg)

Life span: 12–15 years

Diet: Small fish, squid, octopus, shrimp, sea snakes

Angel shark

Squatina squatina

- Angel sharks bury themselves on the sandy seabed, where their colors and patterns help them hide. They lie there, waiting for prey. When prey swims close by, they lunge upward in a surprise ambush attack.

- The flat angel shark is named after its long, winglike front fins, which look like the wings of an angel.

- A wide mouth and strong jaws—lined with rows of sharp, needlelike teeth—help the shark grab and hold slippery prey.

- An angel shark looks as if it has whiskers on its snout. These are called barbels. They help it sense its prey and taste food.

- Young angel sharks have blotches on their bodies that look like eyes. They use these to frighten predators away. The blotches disappear as the sharks become adults.

Fact file

Lives: Northeastern Atlantic Ocean, Mediterranean Sea

Habitat: Sandy or muddy seabeds near coasts

Length: 5 ft (1.5 m)

Weight: 75 lb (35 kg)

Life span: 25–35 years

Diet: Fish, crabs, shellfish, squid

Angel sharks are in danger of becoming extinct. Fishing trawlers catch them by accident in their nets. Wind farms are sometimes built in the areas where baby angel sharks are born, disturbing nursing areas.

Greenland shark

Somniosus microcephalus

- The Greenland shark is a record breaker! It may live for up to 500 years, which is one of the longest life spans of any animal. It keeps growing slowly throughout its life.
- Greenland sharks are the largest fish in the Arctic Ocean. They are the second-largest hunting shark after the great white.
- Female Greenland sharks are at least 150 years old before they have their first pup. This is because they develop so slowly.
- Greenland sharks are one of the slowest-swimming sharks. The seals they eat swim much faster than they do. They may sometimes catch a seal when it is sleeping in the water.
- The Greenland shark will eat almost anything, alive or dead. It hunts when it can, but it also eats a lot of meat from dead animals, such as whales or drowned caribou.
- Some Greenland sharks are almost blind because of a tiny wormlike parasite living on their eyes. They have to use other senses to find food.

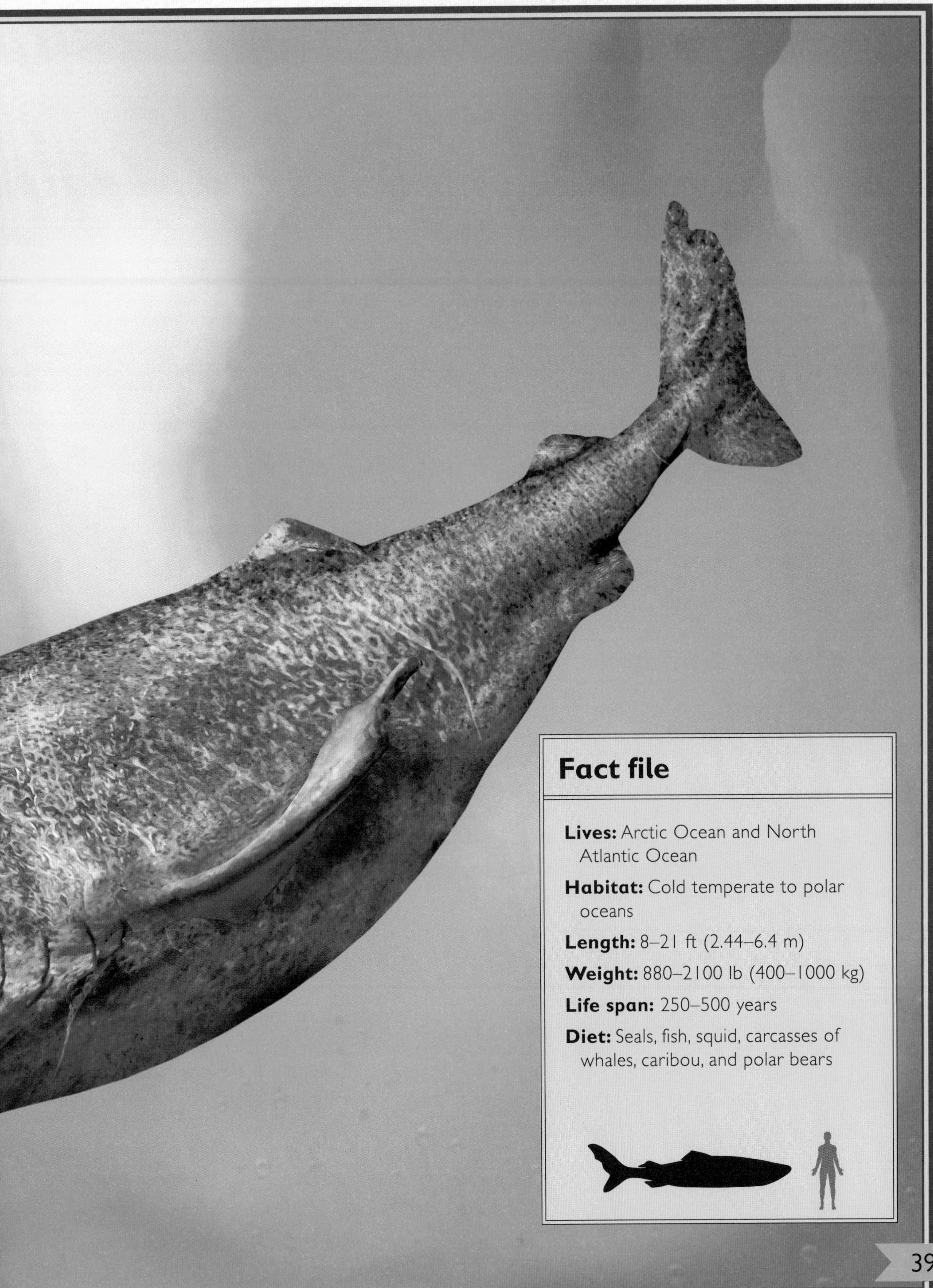

Fact file

Lives: Arctic Ocean and North Atlantic Ocean

Habitat: Cold temperate to polar oceans

Length: 8–21 ft (2.44–6.4 m)

Weight: 880–2100 lb (400–1000 kg)

Life span: 250–500 years

Diet: Seals, fish, squid, carcasses of whales, caribou, and polar bears

Tiger shark

Galeocerdo cuvier

- The tiger shark is one of the most dangerous sharks of all. It will attack anything, including humans. Adult tiger sharks even eat young tiger sharks.
- Tiger sharks are named for their striped markings. These are strongest on young tiger sharks, and help camouflage them from predators, such as other sharks. The stripes fade as they get older.
- The tiger shark is a very strong swimmer. This skilled predator usually stalks its prey and then attacks with a sudden rush of speed when it is too late for the prey to escape.
- Using its sharp eyesight and keen sense of smell, the tiger shark hunts for food at night.

- Tiger sharks are not fussy feeders and will sometimes eat trash, such as cans, bottles, shoes, and tires.

- Like other sharks, the tiger shark has a clever trick for getting rid of things it can't digest. It quickly turns its stomach inside out through its mouth, like someone emptying their pockets.

- Large, powerful, jagged teeth allow the tiger shark to easily slice through tough prey, even the hard shells of sea turtles.

- This shark is the fourth largest in the world. It weighs as much as a large horse.

Fact file

Lives: Worldwide, except Mediterranean Sea

Habitat: Temperate and tropical coastlines, coral reefs, rivers

Length: 10–18 ft (3–5.5 m)

Weight: 900–2000 lb (408–907 kg)

Life span: 15–40 years

Diet: Fish, rays, squid, seals, dolphins, turtles, seabirds, human garbage

Shortfin mako

Isurus oxyrinchus

- The shortfin mako is the fastest shark in the ocean. A torpedo-shaped body and a powerful tail mean it can race through the water as quickly as a car, at speeds of up to 50 mph (80 km/h).

- This incredible athlete makes spectacular leaps right out of the water to catch its prey. It can jump as high as 20 to 30 ft (6–9 m) above the surface—about the height of a two-story house.

- The "mako" part of this shark's name comes from a Maori word that means either "shark" or "shark's tooth." The Maori people live in New Zealand.

- The shortfin mako's skin has flexible, scalelike spikes on its surface. These reduce the drag of the water on its skin, like a swimmer's wet suit. They allow it to slide through the sea faster than any other shark.

- Shortfin makos are able to keep their body temperature warmer than the water around them. This allows them to swim fast over long distances, especially in cooler water.

- These high-speed swimmers burn a lot of energy, so they have to eat plenty of food. They fiercely defend their food, as they cannot afford to lose a meal.

Fact file

Lives: Worldwide, except very cold oceans

Habitat: Open ocean and coastal waters

Length: 13 ft (4 m)

Weight: 1,200 lb (545 kg)

Life span: 29–32 years

Diet: Fish, squid, other sharks, sea turtles, porpoises

Zebra shark

Stegostoma fasciatum

- The long, sleek zebra shark gets its name from the black and white stripes it has when it is young. As they grow, their stripes turn to spots.
- Young zebra sharks have a clever way of fooling predators. They have very long tails and look and swim like banded sea snakes, which are highly poisonous. Predators mistake them for these snakes and stay away.
- A zebra shark's mouth is crammed with 50 to 65 teeth.

Fact file

Lives: Western Pacific Ocean, Indian Ocean

Habitat: Coral and rocky reefs, mangroves, seagrass beds

Length: 8 ft (2.5 m)

Weight: 35–44 lb (16–20 kg)

Life span: 25–30 years

Diet: Sea snails, sea urchins, fish, squid, crabs, shrimp, sea snakes

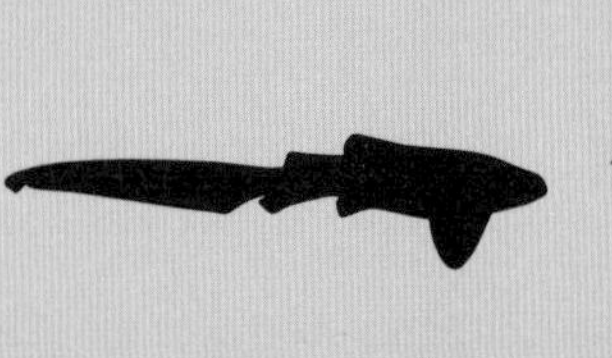

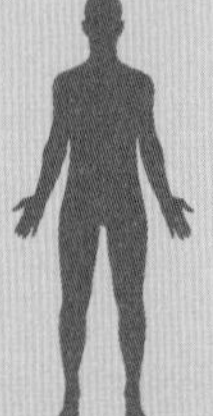

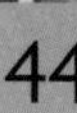

- Short, fleshy feelers, called barbels, on the shark's snout help it sense prey. It also has a flexible body so it can squeeze into spaces where prey hides.

- The zebra shark sucks up its prey in one gulp with its strong mouth muscles. It uses its powerful crushing teeth to smash through the hard shells of crabs, shellfish, and shrimp.

- Female zebra sharks lay up to four egg cases at a time. Fine, hairlike fibers on the egg cases help them stick to rocks and seaweed so that they don't get washed away by waves and currents.

- Zebra sharks are usually gentle with people and will even take food out of a diver's hands. But they may bite if they feel threatened.

Scalloped hammerhead

Sphyrna lewini

- The scalloped hammerhead is named for the notches along the front of its head. These give its head a scalloped, or crinkled, edge.
- Like the great hammerhead, this shark may use the ends of its "hammer" head to pin stingrays to the seafloor. This stops the prey from escaping.
- This hunter can detect prey over a big area. This is because its head is so broad that its eyes, nose, and electrical sensors are widely spaced out.
- Despite their large size, scalloped hammerheads have small mouths and cannot eat prey larger than stingrays.
- Hundreds of these hammerheads sometimes gather in huge schools, or groups. They come together to feed or look for a mate. They may also feel safer in a crowd.
- Scalloped hammerheads "talk" to each other using their bodies. They push against their fellow sharks, shake their heads, spin around, and open their mouths.
- These endangered sharks may become extinct. People have caught so many of them for their skin, meat, liver oil, and large fins, which are used to make shark fin soup.

Fact file

Lives: Worldwide

Habitat: Warm temperate and tropical coastal waters

Length: 5–14 ft (1.5–4.3 m)

Weight: Up to 350 lb (160 kg)

Life span: 25–55 years

Diet: Fish, octopus, squid, stingrays, smaller sharks

Swellshark

Cephaloscyllium ventriosum

- A swellshark balloons to almost twice its size when it is threatened. It curves its body into a U shape and gulps water into its stomach. A predator finds it harder to bite the swollen shark, or to pull it out of a rocky crevice.

- This shark can also puff itself up by swallowing air at the surface. This makes it look bigger and more frightening, and startles predators.

Fact file

Lives: Eastern Pacific Ocean

Habitat: Shallow coastal waters

Length: 35¼–43 in (90–110 cm)

Weight: 9½–17 lb (4.3–7.7 kg)

Life span: 20–35 years

Diet: Small fishes, shellfish, crabs

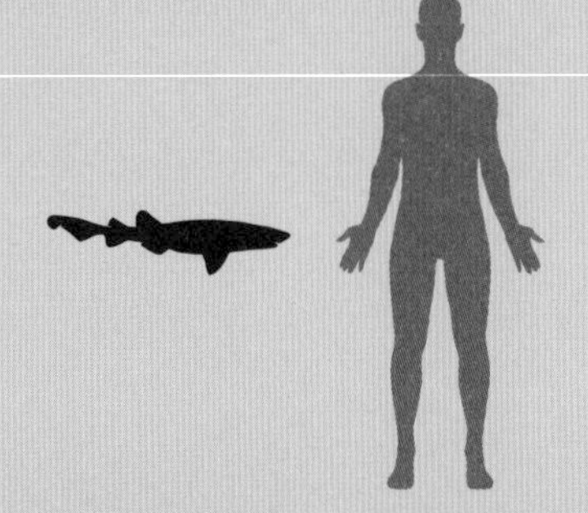

- The swellshark makes a sound like a dog barking as it belches out the water or air it has swallowed. Then it shrinks back to its normal size.
- This patient predator lies motionless on the seafloor with its mouth wide open. It waits for unsuspecting prey to swim in or to be swept in by the water currents.
- A swellshark has 55 to 60 tiny, pointy teeth.
- Swellsharks glow bright green in the dark so that other swellsharks can see them.
- Groups of swellsharks sometimes rest together during the day. They may pile on top of each other like a stack of logs.

Lemon shark

Negaprion brevirostris

- The lemon shark's yellowish back helps it blend in with the sandy seafloor. It is so well camouflaged that prey may not spot it until it is too late!

- This patient nighttime hunter prefers prey that is slow and easy to catch, such as parrotfish and lobsters. It has long, sharp, curved teeth for catching slippery fish.

- During the day, lemon sharks often rest on the seafloor. At dawn and dusk, up to 20 sharks can gather in groups to help each other catch prey. The groups are organized like a wolf pack, with some sharks having a higher rank than others.

- Lemon sharks see well in murky water, but they can also sense the electrical signals given off by objects around them. This sense helps them find their prey.

- At first, lemon shark pups live in a kind of nursery. This is an area where baby sharks will be safe, such as the shallow coastal waters around mangrove tree roots.

- These intelligent, social sharks are now endangered because too many have been caught for their meat, fins, and skin. Scientists are working to help save them.

Fact file

Lives: Atlantic Ocean, Pacific Ocean

Habitat: Shallow water near coasts, river mouths

Length: 8–11 ft (2.4–3.4 m)

Weight: 190-220 lb (85–100 kg)

Life span: 27–30 years

Diet: Fish, rays, crabs, seabirds, other sharks

Pygmy shark

Euprotomicrus bispinatus

- The pygmy shark is the second-smallest shark in the world. It can fit in an adult human's hand. Only the dwarf lanternshark is smaller.
- By day, the pygmy shark lives near the bottom of the ocean. Every night, this little fish goes on a marathon journey. It swims all the way up to the surface waters in search of food.
- These small sharks are fierce predators. They use their large, knifelike lower teeth to catch their prey.
- The pygmy shark's belly glows blue in the dark. This may help it attract curious prey, or camouflage it against the light of the blue surface waters above.
- The tiny pygmy shark has a big head, a paddle-shaped tail, and very small fins on its back.
- The huge, sensitive eyes of the pygmy shark help it see in the darkness of the deep sea.
- Transparent patches of skin above the pygmy shark's eyes allow it to look upward as well as sideways and forward.
- Female pygmy sharks give birth to about eight pups at a time.

Fact file

Lives: South Atlantic Ocean, Indian Ocean, Pacific Ocean

Habitat: Deep ocean and surface waters

Length: 8–10 in (20.3–25.4 cm)

Weight: ½–¾ oz (18.4–23 g)

Life span: 20–30 years

Diet: Krill, small fish, squid

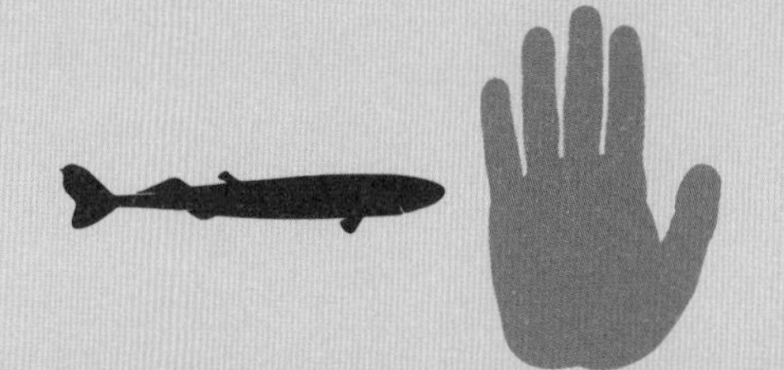

Salmon shark

Lamna ditropis

- The salmon shark is a top ocean predator. It can swim at speeds of up to 50 mph (80 kmh). That's 25 times faster than the average human swimmer!
- Salmon sharks feed mainly on fish such as salmon, herring, cod, mackerel, and sardines. They travel long distances, following great schools of these fish as they make their seasonal migrations.
- Like the great white, the salmon shark can keep its body temperature higher than the surrounding water. This allows it to speed after prey at different depths in the ocean and in colder water.
- Large groups of 30 to 40 salmon sharks sometimes come together to feast on prey.
- A salmon shark has a large, oily liver, which helps it float. Its liver can make up to a quarter of its body weight.
- Female salmon sharks are pregnant for about nine months, which is the same as a human. Every spring, these sharks can give birth to between two and five pups.

Fact file

Lives: North Pacific Ocean

Habitat: Coastal waters and open ocean

Length: 6½–10 ft (2–3 m)

Weight: Over 660 lb (300 kg)

Life span: 17–25 years

Diet: Fish, squid, sea otters, seabirds

Bull shark

Carcharhinus leucas

- The bull shark has a similar shape to a bull, with a stout, muscular body and a short, wide, blunt snout. It head-butts its prey too, just like a bull.
- Bull sharks swim far inland in big, wide, tropical rivers. Some even jump over river rapids, like salmon do, to reach freshwater lakes.
- Huge jaws and large, sharp, jagged teeth give this shark a strong bite. It feeds on almost anything, from fish and squid to dolphins and turtles. This hungry hunter even eats other bull sharks and baby hippos.
- Bull sharks often have small fish called remoras hitchhiking on them. The fish attaches itself with suckers and feeds on skin parasites and food scraps.
- The fierce, powerful bull shark is found in waters close to where a lot of people live. It sometimes attacks humans if it finds them swimming nearby.
- This superfast shark can swim five times faster than an Olympic swimmer, but only for short amounts of time.
- Bull sharks take more time to digest their food when there is not much to eat. This means they can survive for longer if food is scarce.

Fact file

Lives: Worldwide

Habitat: Warm coastal waters, rivers, lakes

Length: 7–11 ft (2.1–3.3 m)

Weight: 200–500 lb (91–227 kg)

Life span: 12–16 years

Diet: Fish, stingrays, squid, turtles, seabirds, dolphins, crabs, sea stars, other sharks

Pyjama shark

Poroderma africanum

- The pyjama shark is named after its beautiful markings, which make it look like it is wearing old-fashioned striped pajamas.
- This long, flexible shark belongs to the catshark family. It is also known as the striped catshark, and has catlike eyes with wide pupils.
- By day, the pyjama shark usually hides away in caves or under rocks. But when it is active in the day, the shark's stripes break up its body shape so that predators cannot see it so easily.

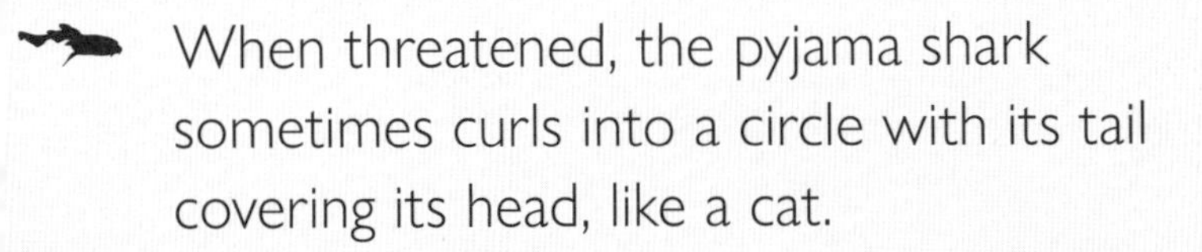

- When threatened, the pyjama shark sometimes curls into a circle with its tail covering its head, like a cat.
- The pyjama shark has sensitive fleshy feelers called barbels on its head. These help it find food.
- The females lay eggs in pairs. Each egg lies safe inside a case called a mermaid's purse. The case has a sticky surface and long, stringy threads to anchor it to seaweed.
- Baby pyjama sharks hatch out of their egg cases after about five or six months.

Fact file

Lives: Southeast Atlantic Ocean, western Indian Ocean

Habitat: Coastal waters, coral reefs, and kelp beds

Length: 2–3 ft (60–95 cm)

Weight: 15–17 lb (6.8–7.7 kg)

Life span: Up to 20 years

Diet: Squid, crabs, shrimp, octopus, worms, fish

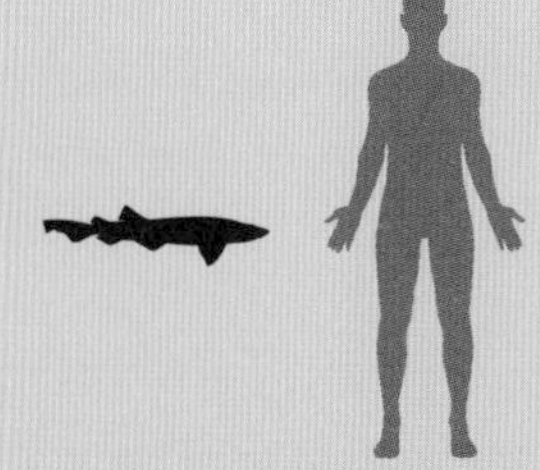

Basking shark

Cetorhinus maximus

- The basking shark is the second-largest shark in the world. It is as long as three small cars! Only the whale shark is bigger.
- This massive shark looks as if it is basking in the sun when it feeds near the surface of the water, which is how it got its name.
- A basking shark sometimes breaches, or leaps out the water, flopping back down with a mega-sized splash. This may help it get rid of parasites on its skin or communicate with other basking sharks.
- Sometimes, basking sharks swim in large groups, called schools, of 50 to 100 sharks. Each school is made up only of males or females.

Fact file

Lives: Worldwide

Habitat: Coastal temperate and Arctic waters

Length: 23–40 ft (7–12 m)

Weight: 6,500–13,000 lb (2,948–5896 kg)

Life span: 50 years

Diet: Plankton

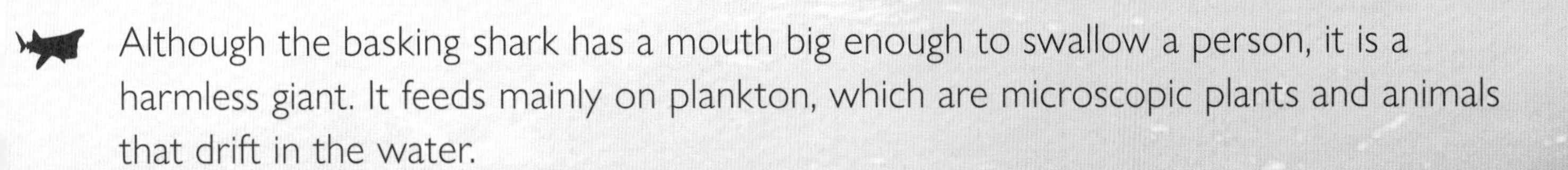

- Although the basking shark has a mouth big enough to swallow a person, it is a harmless giant. It feeds mainly on plankton, which are microscopic plants and animals that drift in the water.

- To get enough to eat, the basking shark filters plankton from the water using slimy spines in front of its gills. Every hour, it filters as much water as there is in an Olympic-sized swimming pool.

Sandbar shark

Carcharhinus plumbeus

- Sandbar sharks prefer to live on smooth, sandy seabeds, which is how they got their name. They are also known as brown or thickskin sharks.
- Some sandbar sharks go on long, seasonal migrations. They swim north in the warm summer and return south when the temperatures cool down.
- Male sandbar sharks migrate in large groups, while females travel on their own.

- Female sandbar sharks do not have pups until they are about 16 years old. They are pregnant for up to a year and have young every two or three years.

- Sandbar shark pups live in shallow water near the coast for about 9 to 10 months. Here, they are protected from attack by larger sharks.

- Too many sandbar sharks have been caught by people for their large fins, flesh, skin, and livers. They are now threatened with extinction.

Fact file

Lives: Western and eastern Atlantic, Mediterrean Sea, Persian Gulf, Red Sea, Indian Ocean, eastern Pacific Ocean

Habitat: Coastal waters, open ocean

Length: 6–8 ft (2–2.5 m)

Weight: 100–200 lb (45–90 kg)

Life span: Over 30 years

Diet: Fish, octopus, crabs, shrimp, rays, snails

Epaulette shark

Hemiscyllium ocellatum

- Epaulette sharks can walk on land! When the tide goes out, they use strong, paddle-shaped fins to clamber about between rock pools, looking for prey.

- This shark can survive in places with very little oxygen in the water, such as rock pools. This means it can feed in places where other fish cannot live.

Fact file

Lives: Coral Sea near northern Australia and New Guinea

Habitat: Coral reefs, shallow coastal waters

Length: 21–42 in (54–107 cm)

Weight: 6¼–11 lb (2.9–5 kg)

Life span: 20–25 years

Diet: Worms, shrimp, crabs, small fish

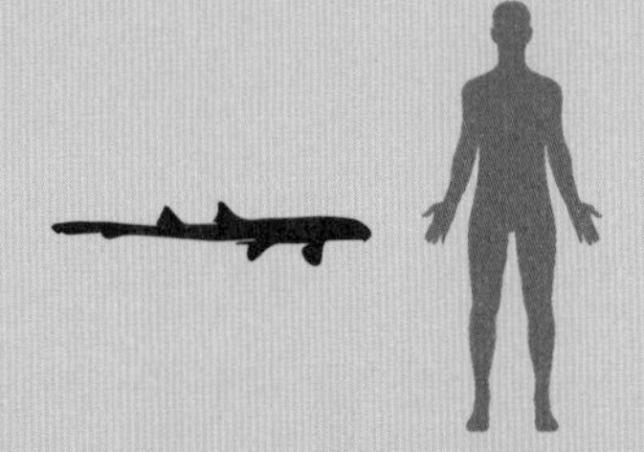

- The two large black spots on the shark's body look like the epaulettes, or shoulder decorations, on a soldier's jacket. Predators mistake the spots for big eyes and stay away.

- The spotted patterns on the epaulette's body help camouflage it in the coral reefs where it lives.

- The epaulette shark can last 60 times longer without oxygen than a person can. To do this, it slows down its breathing and heart rate and uses only the parts of its brain that it needs to stay alive.

Longnose sawshark

Pristiophorus cirratus

- The longnose sawshark has a snout that is one-third the length of its body. Twenty razor-sharp teeth lie on each side of its snout, which looks like a thin, jagged saw.

- This shark shakes its toothy "saw" rapidly from side to side to slash and kill its prey. It also uses its "saw" to dig prey out of sandy seafloors.

- Two long feelers, or barbels, on the shark's snout are sensitive to touch and taste, and the movement of water. They feel for prey buried on the seafloor.

- The sawshark shakes its "saw" to loosen prey buried in the sand then sucks the catch into its mouth. The shark crushes the prey with the 40 to 50 small, thornlike teeth in its top jaw.

- Sawshark pups are born live, not laid as eggs. Their teeth are folded back against their snouts so that they do not injure their mother as she gives birth.

- Sawsharks use their "saws" to defend themselves from larger sharks or to fight with rivals.

Fact file

Lives: Eastern Indian Ocean around southern Australia and Tasmania

Habitat: Offshore waters, deep ocean

Length: 35–55 in (90–140 cm)

Weight: 9½–18¾ lb (4.3–8.5 kg)

Life span: 15 years

Diet: Fish, crabs, squid

Broadnose sevengill shark

Notorynchus cepedianus

- The broadnose sevengill is a skilled predator. It often sneaks up on prey and speeds up at the last minute to grab a meal. This hunting method works especially well in murky water, or at nighttime.

- These sharks sometimes hunt in packs, which helps them catch larger prey, such as seals and dolphins.

- The large, comb-shaped teeth in this shark's bottom jaw are used for tearing and cutting flesh. The sharp, jagged teeth in its top jaw keep a strong grip on slippery, struggling prey.

- Most sharks have five pairs of gill slits on their sides, but the sevengill has seven pairs. Water flows over the gills and out through the slits. The gills absorb oxygen from the water so the shark can breathe.
- The broadnose sevengill belongs to a family of sharks called cow sharks, because they have a chunky body like a cow.
- Broadnose sevengills usually cruise slowly along the seafloor, but they sometimes stick their heads out of the water. This spy-hopping behavior is rare among sharks and may help them to spot prey such as dolphins.
- Sometimes, a broadnose sevengill shark may follow its prey right onto the shore.
- In spring and early summer, females give birth to as many as 82 pups at a time, after a pregnancy lasting 12 months.

Fact file

Lives: Pacific Ocean, South Atlantic Ocean

Habitat: Temperate coastal waters

Length: 10 ft (3 m)

Weight: 130–230 lb (59–104 kg)

Life span: Up to 50 years

Diet: Bony fish, small sharks, rays, seals, dolphins

Leopard shark

Triakis semifasciata

- The leopard shark is named after its spotted skin, which looks like the spotted coat of a leopard.
- This active, strong swimmer often forms schools with other leopard sharks or different shark species such as spiny dogfish or smooth-hound sharks.
- Leopard sharks and spiny dogfish work together to catch anchovies in San Francisco Bay on the California coast.
- Leopard sharks sometimes follow the tide in and out to find prey such as crabs and clams, which are not covered by water at low tide.

Fact file

Lives: Eastern North Pacific Ocean

Habitat: Seabed near shore, estuaries, bays

Length: 4–7 ft (1.2–2.1 m)

Weight: Up to 42 lb (19 kg)

Life span: 20–30 years

Diet: Crabs, fish eggs, worms, octopus, fish, small sharks

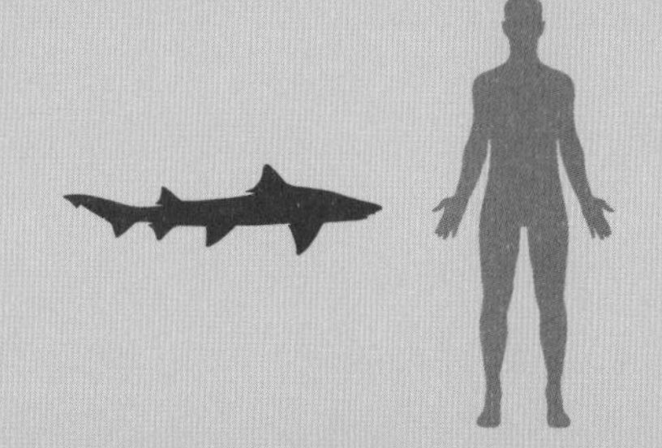

- The leopard shark has small eyes. It does not need big eyes to help it see in the shallow, brightly lit water where it lives.
- Leopard sharks often rest on the seafloor. They pump water over their gills, which absorb oxygen from the water so the sharks can keep breathing.
- Female leopard sharks give birth to as many as 33 pups at a time. The pups take about 10 years to reach adulthood.
- Newborn leopard shark pups have to take care of themselves. They start life in areas of shallow water called nurseries, where they are safer from predators.

Sand tiger shark

Carcharias taurus

- Sand tiger sharks get their name from their large, daggerlike teeth. Although they look dangerous, these peaceful sharks are not usually a threat to people.
- This shark's brownish-gray back helps it disappear into the background of the sandy seafloor. This allows it to sneak up on its prey.
- The sand tiger shark can stay still in the water. It gulps down a mouthful of air from the surface and holds it in its stomach, like a beach ball full of air. This stops the shark from sinking. Sand tigers are the only sharks known to do this.
- Sand tiger sharks sometimes feed together, herding and surrounding schools of fish to make them easier to catch.
- This shark's electrical sense is very useful for detecting the electrical nerve signals given off by prey. It can even find prey buried in the sand at night.
- The sand tiger shark has lots of gaps between its ragged, spiked teeth, which stick out of its mouth. These teeth help the shark keep hold of slippery fish.

Fact file

Lives: Worldwide

Habitat: Warm coastal waters, coral reefs

Length: 6½–10½ ft (2–3.2 m)

Weight: 200–350 lb (91–159 kg)

Life span: 15–30 years

Diet: Fish, rays, crabs, lobsters, squid

Frilled shark

Chlamydoselachus anguineus

- The frilled shark looks like a prehistoric sea monster. It hasn't changed much in millions of years.

- This scary-looking shark snakes through the cold, inky black depths of the ocean, far below the surface. Few people have seen a live frilled shark.

- The frilled shark has six frilly gill slits on either side of its head lined with red fringes. The first pair of gill slits stretches all the way under its throat, like a frilly collar.
- This shark's favorite food is squid. Its 300 razor-sharp teeth face backward to help it hook the squid and stop it from escaping.
- A large mouth and flexible jaws allow the frilled shark to swallow prey whole.
- Female frilled sharks can be pregnant for as long as 42 months—that's three and half years!

Fact file

Lives: Atlantic, Pacific, and Indian Oceans

Habitat: Deep ocean

Length: 4–6½ ft (1.2–2 m)

Weight: 100–200 lb (45–90 kg)

Life span: Up to 25 years

Diet: Squid, octopus, fish, smaller sharks

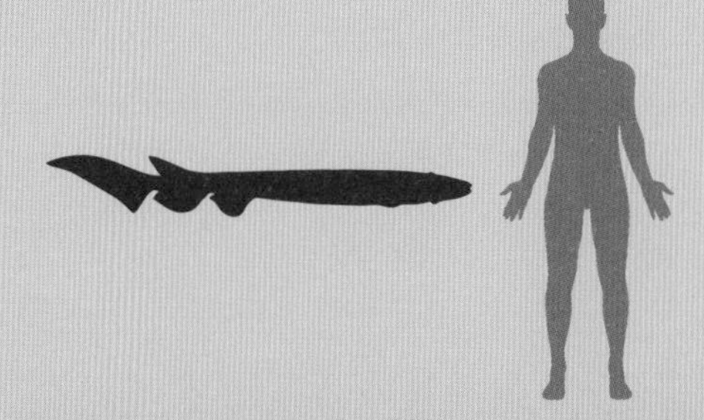

Banded houndshark

Triakis scyllium

- The banded houndshark is named after the dark bands across its body. These markings are strongest when the shark is young but sometimes fade or disappear as it gets older.
- The banded houndshark's teeth are like sharp, pointed blades. They are good for crushing the hard shells of prey such as clams and crabs.
- The houndshark hides away during the day but comes out at night to hunt for food.
- Banded houndsharks usually live alone but sometimes gather in large groups to rest. They may lie piled on top of each other in caves or on the seafloor.
- Baby banded houndsharks grow inside their mother until she is ready to give birth. The mother usually has between 10 and 24 pups at a time, but she can have as many as 42 babies!
- The baby sharks are only 7–8 in (18–20 cm) long when they are born. That is about as long as an adult human's hand. They may not reach their full size until they are eight years old.

Fact file

Lives: Northwestern Pacific Ocean

Habitat: Coastal waters, estuaries, bays

Length: 48–59 in (122–150 cm)

Weight: 44 lb (20 kg)

Life span: 15–18 years

Diet: Small fish, crabs, shrimp, clams, worms, squid, octopus

Spinner shark

Carcharhinus brevipinna

The spinner shark feeds by spinning upward through schools of fish with its mouth wide open. It often shoots right out of the water, spinning around up to three times before splashing back down into the sea.

This agile predator can leap 20 ft (6 m) into the air at speeds of up to 46 mph (74 kmh)—that's twice its own height and twice as quick as the fastest Olympic runner.

Spinner sharks are built for speed. Their slender bodies and long, pointed snouts give them a streamlined shape. This helps the sharks move swiftly through the water after fast-swimming fish.

Fact file

Lives: Atlantic, Pacific, and Indian Oceans; southern Mediterranean

Habitat: Warm, shallow coastal waters, deep ocean

Length: 6–10 ft (1.8–3 m)

Weight: 123 lb (56 kg)

Life span: 15–20 years

Diet: Fish, octopus, squid, cuttlefish, stingrays

- Large groups of spinner sharks travel together in search of smaller fish to eat. They follow schools of fish on their migration journeys through the ocean. That way the sharks always have plenty to eat.

- The narrow, pointed teeth of spinner sharks are made for grabbing slippery prey, which they swallow whole.

- Spinner sharks are not usually dangerous to humans. But they are threatened by people who catch them for their meat, skin, oil, and fins.

Sharks' World

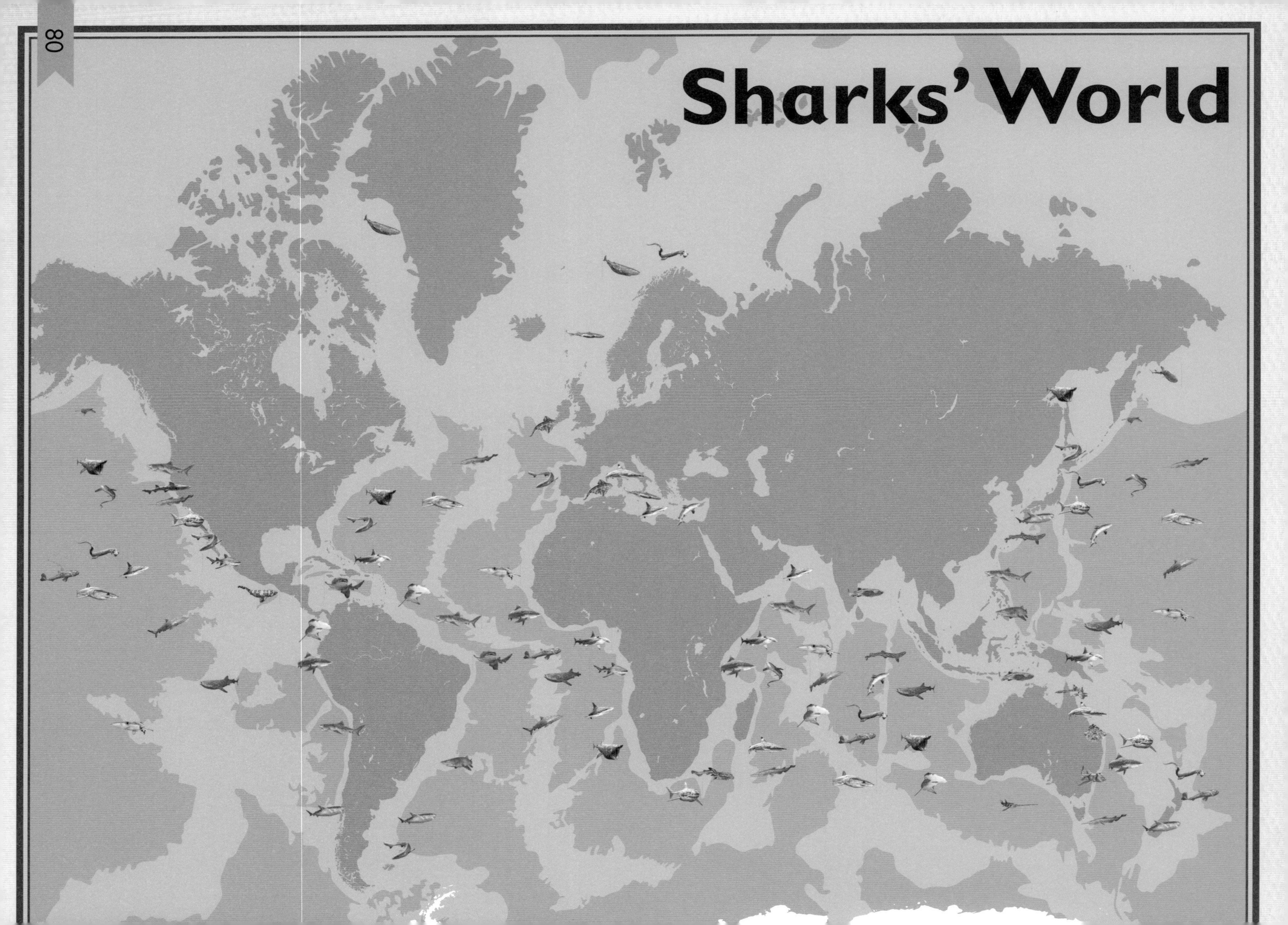